ACHIEVING

Balance in Ministry

PASTORAL QUICK READ SERIES

ACHIEVING
Balance in Ministry

ANTHONY J. HEADLEY

Beacon Hill Press of Kansas City
Kansas City, Missouri

ISBN 083-411-8165

Printed in the United States of America

Cover Design: Paul Franitza

Unless otherwise indicated, all Scripture quotations
are taken from the *Revised Standard Version* (RSV) of
the Bible, copyright 1946, 1952, 1971 by the Division
of Christian Education of the National Council of the
Churches of Christ in the USA.

Permission to quote the following copyrighted version
is also acknowledged with appreciation:

The *New International Version*® (NIV®). Copyright ©
1973, 1978, 1984 by International Bible Society. Used
by permission of Zondervan Publishing House. All
rights reserved.

The *New King James Version* (NKJV). Copyright ©
1979, 1980, 1982 Thomas Nelson, Inc.

Library of Congress Cataloging-in-Publication Data

Headley, Anthony J.
    Achieving balance in ministry / Anthony J. Headley.
       p.   cm. — (Pastoral quick read series)
    Includes bibliographical references.
    ISBN 0-8341-1816-5 (pbk.)
    1. Clergy—Religious life.   2. Clergy—Conduct of life.
 I. Title. II. Series.
    BV4011.6.H43   1999
    248.8'92—dc21
                                  99-32618
                                   CIP

10   9   8   7   6   5   4   3   2   1

Contents

Cultivate Personal Closeness with God • **15**

Follow the Pattern of Jesus • **19**

Recognize Your Limitations • **25**

Interrogate Your *Feel-goods* • **31**

Set Ministry Aspirations Consistent
with Abilities and Limitations • **37**

Avoid Becoming Overextended • **41**

Resist the Pedestal Image • **45**

De-role Yourself Occasionally • **49**

Model Stewardship of Self • **57**

Implement a Realistic View of Ministry • **63**

Make Family Priority a
Foundation for Ministry • **67**

Give a Jethro Person Permission
to Confront You • **75**

Empower Others to Do Ministry • **81**

Remember the Ultimate Power
That Drives Ministry • **85**

Notes • **88**

TAKE TIME TO THINK
TAKE TIME TO PRAY
TAKE TIME TO LAUGH
TAKE TIME TO PLAY
TAKE TIME TO LOVE
AND BE LOVED
TAKE TIME TO GIVE

taken from a sign on the wall
at Mother Teresa's children's home
in Calcutta

Everybody Wants Balance

Balance—it is an elusive ideal and magnificent goal. Most Christian leaders, especially pastors, desire balance in life and ministry, but many would give themselves a failing grade when it comes to achieving it. While ministers hear a lot about self-mastery, discipline, time management, and wholeness, most are caught up in a daily crunch of trying to sort the urgent from the important. At the same time, most pastors are both magnetically drawn and self-judged by Jesus' words to seek first the kingdom of God and Paul's testimony about doing one thing and having learned the secret of contentment.

What a nerve-wracking confusion all this creates for contemporary ministers.

Meet John Almost-Everybody and Elmer Like-Me

Not long ago, I read about a pastor of

7

a large Protestant congregation who re-signed and turned in his ordination cre-dentials. Let's call him John Almost-Every-body. When asked why, he listed several frustrating factors that prompted him to quit ministry for good:

100-hour work weeks

20 straight nights out of the house

2,700 members to care for

Pressure of congregational expectations

Physical stress leading to surgery for a ruptured disc in his neck

Fear of marital problems

Mental and physical exhaustion

Growing emotional drain and sleep-less nights[1]

The oppressing list—time pressures, overload, conflicting expectations, family stress, exhaustion, and self-neglect—is enough to make anyone consider quitting for good. Sound familiar? Many pastors and other Christian leaders struggle with similar pressures. Without balance, spiri-tual renewal, and creative emotional breaks, the result is inevitably burnout, confusion, and loss of focus.

Another effective pastor—let's called him Elmer Like-Me—felt imprisoned by similar frustrations. He gave the following personal report that, with minor adjustments, sounds like hundreds of other pastors I have met in counseling sessions and seminars:

I went to the Institute for Pastoral Psychotherapy, ostensibly for the purpose of enhancing my pastoral skills. Before long it was clear that I was there to work out some deep personal conflicts that manifested themselves in my body, my marriage, my emotional and spiritual life. My wife and I sought marriage counseling. I went into therapy for myself to begin dealing with my depression. I was exhausted, depressed, withdrawn, and irritable. I was physically, emotionally and spiritually depleted. I grew doubtful about my work and felt frustrated and unappreciated. My depression often led to feelings of despair and thoughts of suicide. My thinking became clouded. Sometimes I would sit in my office and be unable to make phone calls or accomplish any reading or writing. My prayer life diminished. I functioned, but I was dying inside. *I did not know it then, but I know it now. I was burned out* [italics mine].[2]

WHAT HAPPENED TO THE JOY?

Reading John Almost-Everybody's and Elmer Like-Me's stories, one wonders how the idealism of youth, motivation of call, satisfactions of service, and joy of partnering with God leaked out of their ministry. Why didn't these two pastors enjoy in relationship and service what the Russian novelist Leo Tolstoy described when he wrote, "One can live magnificently in this world, if one knows how to work and how to love, to work for the person one loves and to love one's work."[3]

For John and Elmer, the devastation of an unbalanced life becomes frighteningly obvious. Burnout inevitably wreaks havoc in all of one's relationships.

But that's not the whole story of what happens when ministers experience burnout and check out of ministry. Such action continues to haunt them vocationally and makes them ask a thousand "what ifs" for the rest of their lives. Some who burn out leave ministry to eventually recover and find their way back. Like John and Elmer, other talented burned-out pastors leave the ministry permanently. Still others continue to serve without the passion that once energized their ministry; they become ministerial robots, doing just enough to get by but hating themselves and their situation. All carry emotional scars for the rest of their days.

It Can Happen to Anyone

Unfortunately, some of the most talented and committed clergy fall victim to burnout because they never find balance and rhythm in ministry. Typically, these pastors put everything—heart, soul, and energy—into ministry. Most are deeply dedicated to the cause of Christ. Losing such persons or having them coast represents an incredible loss to the church.

This situation did not start in modern

times. In Old Testament times as early as Exodus 18, Moses burned the candle at both ends. He pushed himself to the brink of exhaustion. He worked excessively long hours, served a group too large for any one person to lead, and apparently ignored his own health and his family's well-being. He was on the brink of burnout. His problems sound a lot like John's and Elmer's.

BURN OUT, RUST OUT, OR BALANCE?

In my early training for ministry, I believed burnout was the inevitable lot and maybe a badge of honor for God's dedicated servants. Where did I get such a mistaken idea? It came from a Christian leader who loved to pontificate: *"Young men, I would rather burn out than rust out!"* To a rookie, those words possessed a noble, even sacrificial ring—the stuff legends are made of. This philosophy of ministry sounded worthy of imitation. Fortunately, I have since learned another perspective. Rather than communicating noble sacrifice, my leader's words were frighteningly shortsighted.

Are those the only options God gives us—rust out or burn out? Is there some alternative? After examining Scripture, reflecting on my ministry, spending hundreds of hours of counseling, and conversing with many ministers, I am convinced there is a better way.

If we seek to fulfill our ministry—to persevere, to thrive, and to achieve—we need a healthy, satisfying balance in ministry. Balance prevents burnout and confusion. How do we find such balance? Like most exemplary achievements in life, balance is a process that requires frequent return to simple but significant basics. At the risk of sounding overly simplistic, I offer these essential practices for finding stability and enjoying balance in your service to Christ.

IF YOU WILL ASK GOD

WHAT HE'D REMOVE

IF IT WAS HIS LIFE,

HE WILL GLADLY

SHOW YOU.

Bob Benson

1. CULTIVATE PERSONAL CLOSENESS WITH GOD

In his book *Creative Ministry,* Henri Nouwen advises us, "A Christian minister will never be able to be a minister if it is not his most personal faith and insight into life that forms the core of his pastoral work."[4] This insight, easily overlooked in the hustle and daily demands, highlights the critical connection between a minister's spirituality and work. Intimacy with Christ is absolutely essential for ministry just like oxygen is necessary for physical life.

This close connection with God is a pressing necessity for finding fulfillment in ministry. Personal faith and growing relationship with God is the foundation for one's service to others. "Friendship with Jesus, fellowship divine" is how the songwriter described it. But when we fail to keep God in first place, we easily fall into the trap of making ministry an idol. Then we worship our work.

Mistakenly, many ministers think of themselves as being clergy before they think of themselves as being a Christian.

When this happens, ministry activities take priority over being an authentic believer. Being a professional clergyperson becomes the pastor's primary means of relating to God, of thinking about spiritual realities, and of serving the people of God. *Doing* ministry is substituted for *being* Christian—as a result, we have form without substance and activity without empowerment. Then, preaching, public reading of Scripture, praying for others, and providing spiritual direction are done without power and passion.

Being close to spiritual realities is not the same as experiencing them personally. Let's not fool ourselves into believing the spin-off from professional activities nourishes our spiritual lives. To do so is to make the Bible and prayer mere tools of our occupation and to make preaching merely impressive speech. Such a fallacy makes as much sense as a doctor cultivating his own health by reading medical books and performing surgery.

For every believer, including pastors, there is no substitute for intimacy with

God—not even doing ministry. Such closeness comes through practicing the spiritual disciplines. We draw close to the Father, not merely to speak to others about Him, but so God may speak to us. We open our inner being to Him so He may impact our lives in new, refreshing, even imaginative ways.

EXERCISES

Five Ways to Increase Intimacy with God

* Research and read prayers of the Bible.

* Increase the personal dimensions of your study of Scripture.

* Ask an admired person about how to increase closeness with God.

* Check scriptural record about fasting.

* Increase your being as a source for your doing.

**BUT WHEN WE
FAIL TO KEEP GOD
IN FIRST PLACE,
WE EASILY FALL
INTO THE TRAP
OF MAKING
MINISTRY AN IDOL.**

2. FOLLOW THE PATTERN OF JESUS

Intimacy with God empowers ministry. That is why closeness to the Father was such a large part of the earthly work of Christ. His life and ministry demonstrated a constant connection with God and a wholehearted dependence on Him. Even though Jesus was the Son of God, He sought the Father's companionship and counsel before He ministered to others. He is our model and example.

This fact shows in the prologue to Mark's Gospel where the writer shares insight into the vital relationship Jesus cultivated with His Father. In response, following the baptism of Jesus, God honored His Son by sending the Holy Spirit in the form of a dove. Next came the Father's affirmation: "This is My beloved Son, in whom I am well pleased" (Matt. 3:17, NKJV).

The giving of the Spirit is filled with intimacy between Father and Son. Commentators note that in Mark 1:10, Jesus was the only one who saw the heavens open and the Spirit descending. Thus, one might conclude that Jesus and His Father shared a special moment—a moment of incredible reassurance and communication. The scene is a little like married lovers sharing a private nod or telling wink in public. The wink or nod, whether or not seen by others, provides well-understood communication between two people. In the passage, there is an unspoken though public show of intimacy between the Father and the Son.

TWO AFFIRMATIONS

Two clear affirmations also communicate an intimacy between them. First, the Father affirmed Jesus as the Son; in this context, Son stands not for a messianic title but for our Lord's unique relationship with the Father.[5] Here, God rejoices in the relationship—Father and Son. What a picture for us! Our ministry receives empowerment and affirmation from maintaining a close tie with God. Second, God affirmed His pleasure in the Son; a pleasure that springs at least in part from filial obedience. But there is more. God saw in Him all that He intended for His Son.

The private moment, the terms of endearment, the unqualified approval—such closeness paved the way for Christ's ministry. Significantly, only after this close encounter with the Father and the Spirit (Mark 1:9-13), does Christ begin His public ministry. Once again, we see that ministry to others finds a solid foundation and dynamic empowerment in true intimacy and radical obedience to God.

THE EFFECTS OF SPIRITUAL INTIMACY

What does such intimacy do for Christian leaders? It makes us fully aware of the presence and power of God. Perhaps that is the reason, in his prologue, Mark emphasized the Spirit's presence. There, the Spirit confirmed the loving presence of God and the Father's approval of His Son.

If we want God's presence and approval, we must submit completely to *all* the Spirit's leading. For Christ, the Spirit's blessings led Him into suffering. In Mark 1:12, the Spirit drove—the same strong word used for driving out demons—Jesus into the wilderness. Thus, there appears to be a forceful, direct side to the Spirit's activity in the life of Christ. He obediently followed the Spirit's leading into paths of suffering. Like Him, we must respond to both kinds of leading if we will know the presence and the power.

INTIMACY WITH GOD AUTHENTICATES OUR MINISTRY.

People know instinctively when we live close to our Source. We serve with a unique "firsthand experience" because we have witnessed God's supernatural work in our lives. We know the reality we declare, and it shows. But when intimacy with God falls to a low ebb, we become "Sons of Sceva"—those who attempt to minister without the reality (Acts 19:13-16).

Donald Hands and Wayne Fear explain the sad results in *Spiritual Wholeness for Clergy*.[6] They describe clergypersons who become bankrupt through workaholism, alcoholism, burnout, and "carnaling out." All these difficulties have one thing in common: the loss of closeness with God. The heartbreaking result is either alienation from God and/or loss of ministries.

MINISTRY CAN BE HAZARDOUS

Sadly, without intimacy with God, serving in ministry can become a terrible threat to one's soul. John Ortberg, teaching pastor at Willow Creek Community Church, tells about a minister who confessed in one of their meetings: "I don't mean to whine, but I actually found it easier to pursue spiritual health when I was not in ministry."[7] What a sad admission! But even more startling was the fact that nearly every minister in the room agreed.

Let all Christian leaders be warned— doing ministry represents a danger to one's soul. But how can that danger be faced with strength and courage? The apostle Paul offered a remedy for this danger when he wrote: "I pommel my body and subdue it, lest after preaching to others I myself should be disqualified" (1 Cor. 9:27). He advocated radical discipline. He employed the athletic metaphor of a rigorous regimen of training.

For fulfillment in ministry, follow Paul's example—cultivate the spiritual disciplines that refresh relationship with God. Such spiritual rigor helps us avoid being disqualified for ministry.

SELF TALK QUIZ

Please respond to the following statements:

I found it easier to pursue spiritual health when I was not in ministry.
( ) Agree ( ) Disagree

True intimacy and radical obedience are necessary foundations for effective ministry.
( ) Agree ( ) Disagree

Jesus willingly followed the Spirit's leadings into suffering and so should we.
( ) Agree ( ) Disagree

Spiritual rigor helps us avoid being disqualified for ministry.
( ) Agree ( ) Disagree

3. RECOGNIZE YOUR LIMITATIONS

Every human being, including you, has limitations. Ministers are not messiahs or superbeings. Our limitations of body, emotion, and mind demonstrate our finiteness.

Everyone also has limits that are shaped by genetic heritage and life experience. Some seem to have limitless energy; like the Energizer Bunny, they keep going and going. Others tire easily. Physically, everyone needs food and sleep. Emotionally, only a limited amount of pressure can be tolerated. To survive for the long run, every Christian leader must pay attention to his or her unique limitations.

Jesus' ministry supports this "principle of limited resources." In the Gospel of Mark, people are seen as finite creatures circumscribed by their limitations. Mark describes real people who get hungry, tired, and emotionally depleted. They need solitude and time for retreat. All these limitations showed at various times and in many ways in the disciples. Even Jesus experienced these limitations. He recognized these limitations in himself and commanded His disciples to do the same (Mark 6:31-32).

Failure to admit limitations creates crises for a minister. This happens when resources are overtaxed by overuse. No one can do everything. We do not have enough personal resources to meet every demand that anyone thinks up for us. When needs of others are not prioritized and managed, burnout results and crippling frustrations follow. Commitment to rest, retreat, and renewal are absolutely essential if a minister is to function effectively.

You probably remember how Mark 6 deals with the issue of limitations when the disciples felt spent from prolonged work for God. They were hungry and tired. They were depleted emotionally and mentally. The demands had been so immense they did not take time to eat and had no opportunity for rest or renewal.

The disciples' spiritual resources were apparently overtaxed too. This is evident in Mark 6:12-13, which reports that the disciples preached, healed, and cast out demons—activities taking a lot of spiritual resources. With all the demands of the crowds pressing around them, the disciples questioned how they could find time to replenish their spiritual storehouse. Another question must also be asked: How does one continue God's work without returning to its source?

Not many of us can endure pressures like they experienced for long—not if we want to serve effectively. These demands deplete physical energy and drain spiritual resources. They drain us until we become mere miniatures of our former selves. Moses (Numbers 11) and Elijah (1 Kings 19) illustrate what these losses cause. Both are examples of what happens spiritually, physically, emotionally, and mentally when a leader pushes beyond human limits.

Moses experienced a great deal of strain: he ministered to a dissatisfied flock; he labored alone trying to intercede for a complaining people. He made his stress even greater when he allowed himself self-pity for the burden of serving too many people with too many needs. All the pressures finally did him in so much that in Num. 11:11-15, he expressed anger toward God, even blaming Him for his situation. Deeply distraught, he wanted to die.

Elijah's story mimics Moses' dilemma. He, too, struggled with soul-draining pressure as he carried out his ministry. In 1 Kings 19, Elijah feels exhausted after his rousing victory at Mount Carmel. Earlier, he labored heroically against the prophets of Baal. Then his faith was vibrant and he triumphed against great odds. Now he was physically, emotionally, and spiritually depleted. Isolated from human support, he suffered alone. Fearing for his life, he ran in terror from Jezebel. Completely drained, he sat under a broom tree and wished to die. He broke down emotionally just like Moses.

I suspect the disciples, on tough days, felt a lot like Moses and Elijah. After an exhausting tour of duty, they needed rest; they understood what John Wesley observed centuries later that "faith does not overturn the course of nature." Let's realize that all the spiritual vitality in the world cannot overcome human limitations.

Yet many ministers ignore the limitations of being human. All the while, pious words are used to dress up an addiction to work. Sad but true, pastors often justify their superpastor styles with pious talk that attempts to sanitize and legitimize faulty, destructive patterns.

EXERCISE
Limitations and Strengths

* List your strengths.

* List your limitations.

* List your gifts.

* Where is your church limited because you can't do everything?

* Does someone in your congregation need your permission to serve?

* Do you know the gifts of all your church members?

FEEL-GOODS CASE STUDY

Pastor Bill Hiltner frequently fights two pressing battles. He never feels his ministry efforts are good enough. And he often thinks laypeople in his church do not do their best in service assignments. As a result he often lets others know in subtle ways that they could do better. Sometimes he does things himself rather than asking others because he knows he can do it better. His wife Sally tells him that he is a control freak.

Can you analyze the problem and offer solutions? Do you know pastors who have a similar perspective? How can Bill get things done well and at the same time not offend others? Is Bill's commitment to perfect performance pleasing to God?

4. INTERROGATE YOUR FEEL-GOODS

I met a refreshingly honest pastor whose compulsive patterns had him worn thin both emotionally and physically. But in spite of his awareness, this minister pushed himself to do more in his pastorate. No matter what he did, he never felt it was enough. Driven by scripts from childhood, he actually thought his best was not good enough. While trying to do more at church, he sometimes neglected his other duties as husband, father, and student. Things were not going well in any of his responsibilities.

When confronted with his patterns and questioned about their origins, he confessed candidly: *"I pile up the feel-goods."* I understood immediately what he meant. His success fed his ego. The affirmations bolstered his self-worth. And he drove himself to extremes because his self-esteem always needed more stroking. In the process, he pushed himself beyond his limits and was wearing out. When he came to me, he showed signs of exhaustion, burnout, and confusion. His life was frighteningly out of balance.

Not surprisingly, other areas of his life were suffering too. He was having inter-personal problems at home and church. His relationship with God also suffered. In his confusion, he thought of God as a brutal taskmaster whipping him to do more. For this minister, his Heavenly Father had become an incarnation of his earthly father, for whom nothing was good enough. To avoid criticism from his inner critic and to increase his *feel-goods,* he ignored many warning signs.

God does not expect you to serve beyond your limits. I find this reassuring reality in Jesus' words: "'Come away by yourselves to a lonely place, and rest a while.' For many were coming and going, and they had no leisure even to eat. And they went away in the boat to a lonely place by themselves" (Mark 6:31-32).

Right in the midst of promising ministry opportunities, Jesus called His disciples to withdraw for food and rest. Our Lord's call to His disciples sounds like heresy by today's workaholic standards. Many contemporary pastors and other church leaders might have a different order of priorities that urged disciples to do more like: "Strike while the iron is hot!" "This chance will not come again when people clamor to hear from God." "We must seize the moment." "Forget tiredness! The reward is worth the sacrifice." With words like these, many of us have urged believers and pushed ourselves to do more fever-pitched activities. That happens because we do not really understand Jesus.

Let's ask ourselves why Jesus called His disciples to rest and periodic withdrawal from people. The answer is simple: He recognized the disciples' humanity and their limitations. He knew their mental, emotional, and physical resources could be dissipated. And He also knew they would be more efficient after they had been refreshed and renewed.

Though Jesus multiplied bread and fish to meet human needs, He pursues much different strategies with His disciples and us. In Mark 6, He could have performed a miracle and fed the disciples so they were no longer hungry. With a word, He could have healed their exhaustion and cured their fatigue. But He chose another plan. He called them to rest and withdrawal.

By His preferred method of renewal, Jesus spoke a loud message to ministers and others who lead in the contemporary church. His method is simple—acknowledge your limits and care for your needs. Jesus respects the natural limitations that shape our earthly lives, and He expects us to use the renewal resources available to us. As servants of Christ, we must commit to being refreshed in ways that renew us.

Our Lord's strategies are easy to follow. When the disciples hungered, He called them to eat. When they felt tired, He called them to rest. Jesus' ministry demonstrates a balance between action and rest, serving and retreating, community and solitude. What He patterned for His disciples, He wanted them and us to practice.

EXERCISE

"I pile up the feel-goods."

* How do you react to that statement?

* How does that statement refer to your ministry?

* In your church, who do you want to make you feel good?

* How do feel-goods contribute to burnout?

* What is the benefit of time away for rest and renewal?

* What does "community" and "solitude" say to your present style of ministry?

OUR LORD'S
METHOD IS
SIMPLE—
ACKNOWLEDGE
YOUR LIMITS AND
CARE FOR YOUR
NEEDS.

5. SET MINISTRY ASPIRATIONS CONSISTENT WITH ABILITIES AND LIMITATIONS

All ministers need dreams, ideals, and goals. Some want to be great preachers. Some dream of being servant leaders who do great deeds. Others envision being scholarly interpreters of the Bible. Still others imagine being skilled counselors. And some want all these abilities.

Though all these goals may be worthy ideals, they are inevitably shaped by innate limitations—whether emotional, physical, or mental. Let me explain. Some may lack native abilities to become great communicators. Some may tire quickly due to physical limitations. Others may lack emotional qualities needed to become skilled counselors.

Our spiritual gifting can also limit or liberate us. We must rejoice in the fact that God has uniquely gifted us in some way. Some have gifts of preaching or leadership or encouragement. Others exhibit gifts of teaching, faith, and healing. All are not the same. All have limitations. All have incredible possibilities.

The following story explains my meaning. A friend has two relatives who are ministers. My friend enjoys the company of one but is always turned off by the other. What is the difference? The first minister is real, authentic, and winsome. He knows himself, his gifts, and his limitations and labors in ministry with those realities. The other minister always acts like someone else. He has always aspired to be like a televangelist whom he revered. As a result, he mimics his model. He styles his hair like the evangelist, dresses like him, tries to preach like him, and talks like him—all, of course, without the evangelist's success. Since he so identifies with the TV preacher, he has lots of trouble knowing who he is personally. That's my friend's turnoff. He wishes his relative would learn to be himself and appreciate his own gifts and graces.

That's what I mean by limitations and gifts shaping our ideals and dreams—both positive and negative. We are to be comfortable with ourselves, our gifts, our abilities, our opportunities, and our limitations. To be competently fulfilled, we must allow these realities to shape how we do ministry.

EXERCISE

Six-Question Reality Check

Asking yourself the following questions could sensitize you to these important realities:

* What are my physical, emotional, and mental abilities?

* What are the areas where I lack talents and abilities?

* How does my ministry reflect the presence or absence of these spiritual gifts?

* What abilities and gifts do I have that I have never developed?

* Am I devoting time and energy where I have clear gifts?

* Am I primarily working outside my area of giftedness?

TIPS FOR OVEREXTENDED PASTORS

❋ Focus on one task at a time.

❋ Stop telling yourself you do not know how to start—start.

❋ Break big projects into smaller tasks so you enjoy frequent feelings of accomplishment.

❋ Talk yourself out of an attitude of hopelessness—you are not without hope.

❋ This task is too dull and routine. Get started and congratulate yourself when you finish.

❋ Set your own deadline earlier than the actual deadline.

❋ Refuse to allow yourself to procrastinate. It uses up too much energy.

6. AVOID BECOMING OVEREXTENDED

In every ministry there will be times when the leader must stretch to meet unexpected demands and special opportunities. But no pastor can live like that all the time. Try to pace ministry so you do not *consistently* overextend. This will avoid two ministry hazards: One is believing and acting as though you have to do it all. The other error relates closely to the first —it assumes you must meet every human need presented to you. When these faulty assumptions are believed, overcommitting almost always follows.

Overextending sets in motion a stress cycle that is destructive to family, ministry, and self. At the same time, overextending deprives others from using their gifts. And in the overextending process, we often do our work poorly because of our weariness.

Some may think these suggestions limit ministry. Not so. Actually, they expand effectiveness and add years to our service. Knowing our personal strengths and limitations helps maximize our strengths and makes expeditious use of our unique gift-ings. This helps us to endure and grow to serve another day. No one has to burn out and abandon ministry.

EXERCISE

Brainstorm with Yourself

In a free-wheeling self-conversation, consider these questions:

* When was I most overextended?

* How did I correct the situation?

* Do I feel overextended when focus is the problem?

* What is the relationship between overextending and disorganization?

* Do I overextend to meet some inner personal need?

* Who writes my schedule?

* Do I have an inner script from childhood that causes me to overextend?

DO YOU HAVE SYMPTOMS OF BURNOUT?

If you presently have three or more of the following symptoms, you should get professional help and make life changes immediately:

1. Chronic fatigue without a medical reason.

2. Cynicism and hopelessness.

3. Your attitude is "so what?"

4. You are depressed so you do your work as if you were on autopilot.

5. You are impatient and angry with people.

6. Your work performance has slipped so you miss deadlines and forget commitments you make.

7. You are out of focus about your ministry, marriage, and life.

8. You think you are too strong or too smart to experience burnout.

WE DO NOT KNOW
HOW LONG WE
WILL LIVE,
BUT THIS
NOT KNOWING
CALLS US TO
LIVE EVERY DAY,
EVERY WEEK,
EVERY YEAR
OF OUR LIVES
TO ITS FULLEST
POTENTIAL.

Henri J. M. Nouwen

7. RESIST THE PEDESTAL IMAGE

Ministry, by its nature, often causes confusing boundaries. As a result, ministry roles can be confused with personal identity so we think of ourselves as Rev. Jones rather than Sam Jones. The problems greatly multiply when we think ministry is who we are rather than what we do. One consequence of this confusion is that we fail to allow ourselves to be real people who take time and effort to recognize and meet our own needs. One pastor confessed, "I started to believe I was as wonderful as people said I was." However, to live a life of authentic balance, a minister must know where ministry ends and personal identity begins.

In order to function effectively and happily, the balanced Christian leader must understand the relationships, boundaries, and interplay between personhood and ministry. It is the balance question again—the pastor is both a human being and a minister. Ministers are actually ordinary people, not superhuman pastors . . . who see themselves or want

others to see them as having no life, no
concerns, no limitations, or no needs other than ministry.

"Pedestal people" is what I call indi-
viduals who deny traits they have in common with other human beings. They act
like they have no needs. They fool themselves by saying, "I never get tired," "I always enjoy being with people," "I am never tempted," and "I have never known a
moment of discouragement in 10 years."
Such an unreal self-image would be amus-
ing if it did not wreak havoc in the inner
life of the minister and produce pain in
family and church.

How do ministers get into pedestal
thinking about themselves? Sometimes,
the pedestal notion comes with the role
parishioners encourage when they make
us think erroneously that being in ministry gives us some supernatural power or
heavenly insight. Some ministers even as-
pire to a pedestal image; they enjoy the
fictionalized notion of being superhuman
—even with its heavy price. But to enjoy
ministry, to serve effectively, and to be

whole persons, pastors must intentionally step down from the pedestal. They must admit they have needs like every other person. They must be authentic human beings who have been redeemed.

SELF-CHECK
Pedestal Pastors

❋ Have you ever been one?

❋ If yes, did you enjoy it?

❋ How do you check reality?

❋ What do thoughtful laypersons think of pedestal pastors?

❋ If no, how did you avoid it?

❋ What are the ways to prevent it?

LET ALL CHRISTIAN LEADERS BE WARNED —DOING MINISTRY REPRESENTS A DANGER TO ONE'S SOUL.

8. DE-ROLE YOURSELF OCCASIONALLY

This means stepping out of the pastoral role to find authentic, acceptable ways of being human. It means taking opportunities to be ourselves—to cry and laugh, to hurt and rejoice, to work and play. Striving for balance is a lifelong quest, and dropping the role at times helps us reach the goal. Try it. You will find de-roling refreshes and energizes you so you can return to ministry with new zest and increased passion.

Getting out of the role becomes essential for wholeness, especially after an exhausting period of ministry. I picture this effort as a kind of mathematical equation:

limited resources − depleted resources × various demands = needs for retreat and renewal

Check how this happens in Mark 6:30-34 and 6:45-46. In this passage the disciples had recently returned from touring the cities and villages. They were overworked and confused with the death of John the Baptist, faced with pressing crowds and

5,000 plus hungry mouths. Already exhausted, they faced new demands. Jesus called them aside. He gave them an opportunity to de-role that was a necessity to prevent total exhaustion.

TWO MOVEMENTS

For maximum balance, de-roling should be a regular part of ministry. Serving others should be balanced with faithfully caring for personal and family needs. One must always be moving between personal care and ministry functions. In this sense, ministry is done in two movements. In the first movement, the minister takes time for spiritual, physical, emotional, and mental self-care. It means acknowledging the need for intimate others like spouse and children so family becomes a delight rather than mere duty. Then out of this wellspring of strength, the minister moves into the second movement to meet needs of others. The two movements are not detached; they resource and enrich each other.

Though distinct and different, the two

movements form one whole called ministry. Together, they create an inner harmony so the minister becomes a balanced human being who is worthy to be followed because he combines a healthy humanity with his experience with God.

Pastors can de-role through many activities that enhance their God-given personhood, whether spiritual, emotional, mental, or physical. Explore new ways of prayer and Scripture reading. Read the devotional giants.

Emotionally, de-roling can come through strengthened relations with your spouse, with a friend, or with a support group. Often ministers keep relationships with children and spouse as a showcase for ministry where family is viewed as an example for church and community. Resist the showcase silliness. Family relationships allow opportunities for de-roling so you are Dad or Mom rather than pastor or minister. Develop strong family ties as a gift to yourself and the church.

Mentally, we can care for ourselves through reading and other stimulating intellectual activities. Join a discussion group or take a college course outside your professional interest—try art or computer technology. Spend time with people who see the world different from you. Thinking new ideas helps a pastor resist the temptation to die mentally at midlife. Sharpen your skills of rigorous thinking about life and faith.

DE-ROLING HELPS OTHERS

In addition to the benefits it provides the individual, de-roling often has a positive impact on others. I cannot forget the reaction of a new student when she saw me in shorts playing floor hockey in the seminary gym. It was like a light went on in her mind when she realized I had a life outside the classroom. Now, in her eyes, I had become a fuller person whose life was more than my teaching ministry role.

I have seen the same reaction toward other professors when students discovered their teachers were husbands, wives, fathers, mothers, poets, athletes, musicians, writers, or preachers. I suppose up to that point, students think of us as one-dimensional professionals. Seen in this new light, the instructor becomes an authentic, real person. Such a discovery encourages a softening, an acceptance, and an identification. On the contrary, superhuman people are aloof, otherworldly, and lonely. They may be admired but always at an unapproachable distance.

De-roling provides similar benefits to ministers. The pastor becomes human to parishioners—someone who is approachable and so much more than a righteous symbol of God. Once parishioners are allowed to see your human side, they feel more at ease around you. For them, you become an understanding, caring friend who knows life like they live it. Rather than losing face or status, the minister finds increased acceptance and enjoys wonderful new opportunities for service. Being fully human never diminishes us. Neither does it stifle ministry. On the contrary, allowing ourselves to be authentic human beings enlarges effectiveness and gives an incarnational dimension to our impact on others. Seeing their minister's grace-shaped humanity is a strength laypeople appreciate and value.

JESUS SHOWED HIS HUMAN SIDE

Jesus de-roled himself by showing His human side. One of the most inspiring examples of Jesus demonstrating His human side is found in John 21 after the Resurrection. On that early morning, Jesus was walking along the seashore. I like to think His sandals were off and wet sand trickled between His toes as He reveled in the creation. He called to His disciples who were out fishing. And when they got to shore, they found Him cooking fish on a roaring fire.

Why is this incident intriguing to us? Perhaps the last thing we might expect of the resurrected Christ is to find Him dabbling in mundane things like a fish fry. But we see Him in this passage giving continuing attention to ordinary, common human needs. We see Jesus caring for His famished disciples. I do not think I am stretching the passage too far when I suggest we can learn from Jesus on how to get out of our ministry roles and address our human needs.

High among all the ways to produce balance and fulfillment is what you do to become a real person who does authentic pastoral ministry well.

WRITE YOUR OWN PRESCRIPTION

* How does the de-role idea fit your style of ministry?

* List ways you could de-role that would give you a more authentically human image in the community and church.

   1.

   2.

   3.

   4.

   5.

* Discuss the de-role concept with your spouse. What kind of reaction did you receive?

PUT FIRST THINGS FIRST AND WE GET SECOND THINGS THROWN IN: PUT SECOND THINGS FIRST AND WE LOSE BOTH FIRST AND SECOND THINGS.

C. S. Lewis

9. MODEL STEWARDSHIP OF SELF

I heard a radio preacher disparage stress management as "new age fads." Though badly misinformed, he caused me to think carefully about biblical foundations for self-care. After much reflection, I am thoroughly convinced that God calls us to live as faithful stewards of all He places in our hands. This stewardship goes beyond money to how we manage our spirits, bodies, and emotions. All that I have said so far in this book involves stewardship of our spirits, our humanity, our roles and needs—a total-being way of thinking about stewardship.

Clergy should exemplify total-being stewardship as a response to the gifts God entrusts to them. Just as the Father expects careful management of our treasure, He desires diligent care of our entire being. You remember how the apostle Paul instructed the Corinthians that they were God's temples, which were pure and holy. If they profaned this human temple, they would bring God's judgment upon themselves (1 Cor. 3:16-17). I believe this threat of judgment reflects God's high opinion of the human temple. Elsewhere in the same letter, Paul wrote: "Do you not know that your body is a temple of the Holy Spirit within you, which you have from God? You are not your own; you were bought with a price. So glorify God in your body" (6:19-20).

Evidently, Paul believed we please God by keeping our bodies holy. Therefore, he called the Corinthians to exert spiritual care and dedication to live holy lives—this is spiritual stewardship. Given this high view of the body, Paul would doubtless support other forms of temple care too.

Taking these teachings to heart means developing an attitude of persistent care of our whole self. By all means, this includes intentional diligence to keep oneself holy. But it must also mean practicing appropriate care of our bodies, minds, and emotions. To neglect these is to fail to live as good stewards.

Stewardship of self involves more than our response to God. It is something important we do for ourselves. Ministers must practice good stewardship habits that produce personal health and emotional well being. Moses failed miserably in total-being stewardship when he overextended himself. He was wearing himself out and his effectiveness was starting to wane. Jethro saw that and shared his observations with Moses. Modern clergypersons often learn a similar lesson with much pain. Before they realize it, they are exhausted and burned out—spiritual, emotional, and physical wrecks. They feel miserable, desperate, and frightened.

Another dimension needs to be examined—a balanced pastor does more effective work than an exhausted, overcommitted Moses could do. To overextend ourselves means those in the pew get shortchanged. To quote a Doonesbury cartoon line, *"Highly stressed, chronically fatigued employees cannot give their best."* That is especially true for ministers. Often the best gift a pastor can give a congregation is the gift of a balanced, rested, fully

functioning, redeemed human being—
that authentic stewardship of ourselves.

Moreover, parishioners seldom see living examples of total-being stewardship, how to handle all of life in a sacred way. They need models to show them how to respect the human temple God has given them. As usual, they are more likely to follow what we do than what we say. Let's clean up our act and show them balance and wholeness. Let's stop burning the candle at both ends. Let's show them an example that questions the hustle-bustle life that characterizes so many people in the pew.

Try implementing the first-things-first priorities of Jesus and demonstrate the importance of the Sabbath in your own lifestyle. Such stewardship of self will create balance for you and provide a wonderful pattern for your parishioners.

REFLECTIONS

The best gift a pastor can give a congregation is the gift of a balanced, rested, fully functioning, redeemed human being.

( ) Agree   ( ) Disagree

True at present in my ministry.

( ) Agree   ( ) Disagree

Needs to improve in my ministry.

( ) Agree   ( ) Disagree

I know specific ways to improve.

( ) Agree   ( ) Disagree

FOR JESUS,
MINISTRY OFTEN
INVOLVED A
PRIVATE RETREAT
TO BE
WITH GOD.

10. IMPLEMENT A REALISTIC VIEW OF MINISTRY

In stress and burnout seminars, I ask pastors to define ministry. They invariably define it in other-centered categories. They say things like "Ministry is serving others." "Ministry is what you do for others." Rarely do I hear a definition of ministry that allows a place for self-care. The assumption leads to a deceptive conclusion—if ministry means what one does for others, care for oneself doesn't count.

Several unfortunate consequences follow from this misunderstanding. Typically, it leads to becoming completely absorbed in serving others. As a result pastors take underresponsibility for themselves. Then because of overfunctioning, self-imposed responsibility, many clergypersons justify putting family and self on hold.

Not surprisingly, such an inaccurate view produces feelings of false guilt. A pastor friend enjoys swimming, yet he allows an artificial sense of guilt to stop him from going to the beach. He fears that if church members saw him at the beach, they would think he was "goofing off." Thus, he gave up a healthy pastime because of faulty reasoning that caused counterfeit guilt.

Another example comes from a seminar where I spoke about self-care. At the end of the session, a middle-aged minister said: "Thanks; the next time I go to the gym, I won't feel guilty." Sadly, this faithful pastor felt guilty every time he went to the gym. Why? Because in his mind, he stopped doing ministry when he went to the gym. He mistakenly thought he was cheating the Lord by taking care of himself. What a distorted idea!

Clergy need a more balanced concept of ministry than a choice between serving others and being whole persons themselves. Both are needed and possible. But where does one find such a balance? Again, Jesus shows us how. His pattern of personal ministry before serving others is repeated across Mark's Gospel and in other New Testament references. For Jesus, ministry often involved retreat to be with God—alone or with the disciples. In fact, this was a resource for ministry for others. That's why Jesus' emphasis is retreat before action.

No wonder Jesus called His disciples aside to refresh and renew themselves (Mark 6:31-32). His command makes no sense if ministry is always others-centered. Serving oneself is as much a part of ministry as serving others.

EXERCISE

Self-assessment

Frequently   Sometimes   Never

* I consistently review the meaning of ministry.

* I shape my ministry activity according to my understanding of ministry.

* I share my view of ministry with key lay leaders.

List three actions to give you greater balance:

**TAKE TIME TO
BE HOLY.
SPEAK OFT
WITH THY LORD;
ABIDE IN HIM ALWAYS,
AND FEED
ON HIS WORD.**

William D. Longstaff

11. MAKE FAMILY PRIORITY A FOUNDATION FOR MINISTRY

Besides ministering to self, one must care for family. In my opinion, service to family is ministry. Notice that I call it ministry—not a distraction, not family time, not duty, not responsibility, not example, but ministry.

Understanding this concept relieves another artificial guilt that comes from giving proper attention to family. To avoid those pangs, pastors sometimes push family concerns to the back burner. Some even promise their spouse, their children, and themselves that they will do it later, but later never seems to arrive. This all-too-common dilemma causes great pain for mates and children.

I can't forget the painful, distressed response of a seminary spouse who attended a seminar I led. In that seminar, I defended time with family as ministry. At the end, this young woman thanked me for that insight and, with tears rolling down her cheek, asked: "Who is telling this to our husbands?" It seemed that she had already experienced deprivation from being "in ministry." Her student/minister husband was acting out his misperception that time with family was not ministry.

GOD WANTS FAMILY CARE

Let's be absolutely clear: God does not want any believer to neglect his or her family. Neither does God want any believer to miss the satisfactions that a happy Christ-centered home gives each member of that family. Neither does God want any believer to give so much prominence to marriage and family that he or she cannot be effective in his or her line of work.

Given such widespread misunderstanding in this area, we should not be surprised that many clergy families feel neglected. Many parsonage kids and mates report being left out as their parent/minister focuses on others. Such an out-of-balance situation generates anger toward God, the church, and the ministry.

Some time ago I heard from a professional colleague about some unpublished survey data on stress in clergy families. My friend reported that many spouses and children have an overload of repressed anger. They feel a quiet but seething anger at the church for robbing them of a spouse and parent. In the study, most often the neglecting pastor was male.

CHURCHES WANT FAMILY CARE

These common practices do not necessarily reflect pastoral belief but result from mismotivated pastoral practice.

Let us be realistic to understand that few churches expect their ministers to neglect their families. Fair-minded people will admire a pastor who gives family priority. The problem, then, is with us—we often talk better than we act. We live like Sally Forth, the cartoon character, who sits at her dining room table consumed with office work. Hillary, her teenage daughter, was getting a clear message: "There's nothing more important than work." Sally corrects her daughter: "Family is way more important than work." But in the next frame, Sally is stunned into silence when she realizes the discrepancy between her words and actions. Though she affirmed family as having higher priority than work, her actions communicated just the opposite.

Clergy are sometimes like Sally when they become consumed with ministry to the exclusion of family. In an article published several years ago, John Scanzoni labeled this kind of minister as a "sect-type clergy." Pastors in this category view family as a competitor to ministry. Family is considered a distraction. For this type pastor, when conflict arises between home and church, ministry always wins. Then the minister becomes so consumed with serving others that marriage and family relationships and pleasures become excluded.[8] These clergy are ministry addicts. That's right—addicts.

Whether through chronic absence or addiction to ministry, we send this message: "Ministry to others is more important than my family." The cartoon had a good ending when Sally drops her work—actually calling it junk—and cares for her daughter's need. In the final frame, the daughter, with a smile of triumph, said: "Mothers come preprogrammed. You just need to know which buttons to push."

What an insight for pastors; though we never want to call our work junk, we must realize that holistic, balanced ministry actually programs us to be good parents and good spouses. I believe God intends for ministry and family to complement and enrich each other.

Is It Ministry or Addiction?

Ministers caught in the web of addictive ministry styles must reprogram themselves to intentionally prioritize family needs. When we do, we make a startling discovery that some other time-consuming tasks are not really as important as we thought. That's what many veteran ministers say when they reflect over years of pastoral service.

There's an important lesson for pastors. Rather than distracting from ministry, family gives us splendid relief from debilitating stress, provides affirming support, and equips us with a reality check about what we assume about the real world. All these benefits can help clergy preserve and find fulfillment in ministry.

Everything psychologists and medical doctors know about stress supports this concept. Invariably, a supportive relationship with family helps everyone cope more effectively with stress. If we neglect our marriage and our children, we harm them and rob ourselves.

EXERCISE

What I Believe About Family and Ministry

Evaluate these statements and discuss with spouse.

T F 1. Service to family is ministry.

T F 2. God does not want any believer to neglect family.

T F 3. My spouse and/or children feel anger toward the church.

T F 4. Ministry to others can become an addiction.

T F 5. Supportive family relationships help us cope with stress.

CONSIDER CONSEQUENCES

Most of us have been warned about the negative consequences of some actions. Why not consider the positive consequences of giving family a high place in ministry. Are you committed to making the following consequences come true for you and your family:

* Children have happy memories of growing up in a pastor's family.

* Spouse sees benefits and perks for the family.

* Memories are made.

* Sense of fulfillment as family gladly teams in ministry.

* You have happy memories in place of regrets when children are grown.

* Balance makes home more meaningful for all family members.

* Church members are inspired by seeing your family as patterns for Christlikeness.

NO DELEGATION IS COMPLETE UNTIL THE ASSIGNMENT HAS BEEN DEFINED, THE PERSON RESPONSIBLE NOTIFIED, AND THE DEADLINE SET.

R. L. Mackenzie

12. GIVE A JETHRO PERSON PERMISSION TO CONFRONT YOU

Ministers live in public view. We experience subtle encouragements that make us believe we are indefatigable and indispensable. Caring, counseling, preaching, and leading often endear us to people. Weddings and funerals tie us to people at significant moments in their lives. So they applaud our efforts. They affirm us and we feel important. Sometimes church leaders and key laypersons even laud our driven tendencies and exhausting schedules. All this adulation sometimes drives us to do more and to push past limits. As we "pile up the *feel-goods*," we can become blinded to our tendency to overfunction.

That is when and why we need a Jethro person. We need someone like Moses' father-in-law who refuses to buy into a glorified image that an overcommitted ministry brings. We need someone to lovingly confront us with the foolishness of our ways.

A Jethro person provides social support. By social support, I mean a network of persons who love, value, and esteem us.

Sometimes a Jethro person is needed to share our successes and joys. At other times, we need our Jethro as a caring presence to support us in times of failure and hurt. But at still other times, we need a Jethro to challenge our reality, style, biases, and assumptions. Then, candor is more important than flattery. Though this latter Jethro function may not be easy to receive, we need it. Listening to Jethro often means the difference between burnout and lasting achievement.

BURNOUT HARD TO RECOGNIZE

Of all the people around Moses, only Jethro confronted his self-destructive leadership practices. Perhaps others close to Moses, like Aaron and Miriam, saw it but didn't do anything to correct it.

What is even more astounding is Moses' lack of self-understanding. He created his schedule and was so involved in fulfilling his unrealistic commitments that he was oblivious to what was going on inside himself. He ignored his exhaustion and tried to work harder and longer. This action demonstrates a confusing reality—the one suffering from symptoms of burnout is often oblivious to the dangers until it's too late.

WORN-OUT PASTORS WEAR OUT PARISHIONERS

All these reasons and more are why every minister needs a Jethro person. Jethro sized up the situation quickly and saw Moses wearing out under the load. Jethro also realized Moses' leadership would eventually drain the people; he knew intuitively, "Worn-out pastors wear out parishioners." Thus, Jethro called Moses to a new strategy that would insure his own well-being and the Israelites' future.

It takes ability to think and courage to be a Jethro person to a pastor. Such courage must spring from a loving concern for the pastor's welfare and ministerial effectiveness. Because of that love, these persons dare to speak.

In fact, they push for health and wholeness even at the price of inciting anger. It requires that the pastor give the Jethro permission too. It is nearly impossible to be a

Jethro if the minister resists. That's the risk Jethro faced when he confronted Moses. How dare a nomad from the desert question this giant in Israel?

GET PAST THE DISCOMFORT

Every minister needs those who care more about our well-being than our fragile feelings. Unfortunately, because of insecurities, many pastors surround themselves with persons who tell them only what they want to hear. That's a self-destructive mistake.

But where does a pastor find his or her Jethro? Many have a ready-made Jethro person in their mates. Spouses are quick to spot starting signs of stress and the first symptoms of burnout. Courageously, they should speak out and be listened to. Shortsighted ministers disregard spousal concerns to their own detriment.

A Jethro person can sometimes be found in a spiritual mentor or through an accountability group. A member of Kentucky's 1998 NCAA championship team recently started a Christian speaking ministry, and because of his basketball fame, his speaking engagements have mushroomed. He formed a group to whom he makes himself accountable. This group looks out for his welfare, including helping him keep his ego in check. They remind him to keep close to the Lord and to keep his priorities straight. Every minister should be as wise as this young athlete.

Sometimes a caring parishioner may be recruited to serve as the pastor's Jethro. Some thoughtful people in the pew are painfully aware of a pastor's misplaced priority and back-breaking workload. I have a minister friend who has a Jethro woman in his congregation who is also a childhood friend and a member of his church. Having grown up together, they know each other well. This lady, not intimidated by his growing popularity, reminds him regularly of his need for self-care. Judging from the pastor's conversations with me, he appreciates this Jethro person. However a Jethro person is discovered and encouraged, every pastor needs one.

EXERCISE
Finding Your Jethro

* Make a list of people you might enlist to be your Jethro.

* Make a list of what would keep you from giving attention to your Jethro.

* Make a list of why you need a Jethro.

13. EMPOWER OTHERS TO DO MINISTRY

Some pastors try to act like Moses because they enjoy a reputation of being a "superminister." Nothing wrong with Moses' intentions; he just did too much. In our time, the title "superminister" describes one who attempts to do everything. It is a mistaken practice that drains a pastor, stymies gifts of laypeople, and puts a limiting lid on a congregation's accomplishments for Christ. Such a pattern of leadership controls a church rather than equipping persons for ministry. It limits what gets done by the energy, vision, and skills of the pastor.

What's the solution? In a word—it's delegation. In Kingdom efforts, delegation means trusting another with some significant task or ministry. It's the way a minister empowers others.

When Moses complained about his overload (Num. 11:11-15), God directed him to share ministry. The passage reads: "And the Lord said to Moses, 'Gather for me seventy men of the elders of Israel, whom you know to be the elders of the people and officers over them; and bring them to the tent of meeting, and let them take their stand there with you. And I will come down and talk with you there; and I will take some of the spirit which is upon you and put it upon them; and *they shall bear the burden of the people with you, that you may not bear it yourself alone*" [emphasis added] (vv. 16-17). In similar fashion, Jesus called His disciples to share His mission rather than carry the full load himself (Mark 6:7-13).

Delegation accomplishes much. It allows leaders more time to do what only they can do. It also eases their burdens. It allows parishioners to develop and use ministry skills in the life of the church. It helps transform parishioners from spectators to participants. Delegation infuses vigor into congregational life and increases morale.

Ministers who delegate must stay involved with laypersons; this requires making support available—like mentoring, training, resources, authority, and encouragement. In short, effective delegation empowers people and multiplies ministry.

**EVERYONE HAS
86,400
SECONDS A DAY.
HOW YOU
USE THEM
DETERMINES THE
QUALITY OF
YOUR LIFE.**

I

WILL BUILD

MY

CHURCH,

AND THE GATES

OF HADES WILL

NOT

OVERCOME IT.

Jesus (Matt. 16:18, NIV)

14. REMEMBER THE ULTIMATE POWER THAT DRIVES MINISTRY

Ministers, above all else, must always remember that supernatural power is what makes ministry effective. God provides empowerment; this fact saves a pastor from exhausting excesses. When this reality is forgotten, the Christian leader labors as if ministry depended only on his or her human efforts.

Then without much forethought, the pastor starts to behave like a pseudomessiah, without the resources of the real Messiah. In a sense, trying to be self-styled messiahs grows out of a grossly inaccurate understanding of ministry. That is, we forget that a pastor is a representative of Christ and not Christ. We are Christ-bearers but not the Christ. This fallacy is sometimes called "playing messiah." That's all it is—*playing* messiah.

However, such playacting produces dire consequences. Messiah-like, we try to meet everyone's needs and exhaust ourselves by trying to live in a manner that's not possible for us.[9] We start to think we know more than others and are not capable of errors or mistakes.

How does this truth about ultimate power free us? When we realize God's enablement is the one indispensable factor in ministerial effectiveness, we learn to lean on Him more. He can get along without us, but we cannot get along without Him. We are mere vessels for God's use. When we seriously apply this truth to ministry, we rest in confidence that God supplies the resources.

Do you desire for your ministry to be effective over the long haul? Do you want to avoid burnout? Do you wish to "finish your course with joy"? Do you seek genuine balance in ministry and satisfaction in ministry? Then try to follow these guidelines:

> Cultivate personal closeness with God.
> Follow the pattern of Jesus.
> Recognize your limitations.
> Interrogate your *feel-goods*.
> Set ministry aspirations consistent with abilities and limitations.

Avoid becoming overextended.

Resist the pedestal image.

De-role yourself occasionally.

Model stewardship of self.

Implement a realistic view of ministry.

Make family priority a foundation for ministry.

Give a Jethro person permission to confront you.

Empower others to do ministry.

Remember the ultimate power that drives ministry.

Notes

1. Ken Garfield, "A Minister Leaves Flock to Tend Family, Self," *Charlotte Observer,* July 11, 1994.

2. Benjamin W. Pratt, "Burnout: A Spiritual Pilgrimage" in Robert R. Lutz and Bruce T. Taylor, eds., *Surviving in Ministry* (New York: Integration Books, © Taylor Manor Hospital, 1990), 108.

3. Quoted by Alan Loy McGinnis, *The Balanced Life* (Minneapolis: Augsburg Fortress Press, 1997), 9.

4. Henri J. M. Nouwen, *Creative Ministry* (New York: Image Books, 1971), xxiii.

5. Craig S. Keener, *The Spirit in the Gospels and Acts* (Peabody, Mass.: Hendrickson Publishers, 1997), 57.

6. Donald R. Hands and Wayne L. Fear, *Spiritual Wholeness for Clergy* (Washington, D.C.: Alban Institute, 1993).

7. John Ortberg, "What's Really Behind Our Fatigue," *Leadership Journal,* Spring 1997, 108.

8. John Scanzoni, "Resolution of Occupational-conjugal Role Conflict in Clergy Marriages," *Journal of Marriage and Family Therapy,* 1965, 27 (2).

9. Benjamin C. Johnson, *Pastoral Spirituality* (Philadelphia: Westminster Press, 1988).